managing TIME

MANAGEMENT SERIES FROM NEW DAWN PRESS

Managing Leadership

Managing People

Managing Sales

Managing Time

Managing Stress

Managing Projects

Managing Text Messaging

managing TIME

Y C Halan

Sterling Paperbacks

STERLING PAPERBACKS
An imprint of
Sterling Publishers (P) Ltd.
A-59, Okhla Industrial Area, Phase-II,
New Delhi-110020.
Tel: 26387070, 26386209; Fax: 91-11-26383788
E-mail: mail@sterlingpublishers.com
www.sterlingpublishers.com

Managing Time
Copyright © 2005, Sterling Publishers Private Limited
ISBN 978 81 207 6572 6
Reprint 2006, 2007, 2008, 2011

All rights are reserved.
No part of this publication may be reproduced, stored in a retrieval system or transmitted, in any form or by any means, mechanical, photocopying, recording or otherwise, without prior written permission of the original publisher.

Printed in India
Printed and Published by Sterling Publishers Pvt. Ltd.,
New Delhi-110 020.

Contents

Introduction	7
Have a Day of 48 Hours	9
Time Management Skills	21
Improve Your Time Management	38
Time Wasters	46
Tips for Saving Time	58
Check Your Time Management Efficiency Quotient (TMEQ)	85

Introduction

Sudha Murty, wife of N R Narayan Murty, is a busy woman. She plays different roles and leads an extremely busy life—lecturing, writing, working, accompanying her husband all over the world, besides a lot of social work and housework. How is she able to accomplish all that in twenty-four hours? "Good time management," is her answer.

The idea of time management has been in existence for more than hundred years. Unfortunately the term "time management" creates a false impression of that a person has control over time. Time cannot be managed as it is beyond the power of any human being. We can only manage ourselves to get the best out of the time we have at our disposal.

Time management, in fact, is self-management. It is interesting that the skills we need to manage others are the same we need to manage ourselves: the ability to plan, delegate, organise, direct and control.

Have a Day of 48 Hours

Time and money are both extremely important in business. Yet, most of us tend to give a lot more specific thought as to how to spend our money. How we spend our time is seldom given importance. We only think of in terms of "What am I going to do today?" or "What should I do tomorrow?"

Most of us forget that just as a well-run business should carefully develop a strategy to determine how to spend its money, an effective business person, or for that matter anyone who is working for money, should carefully develop a strategy to determine how to use his or her time. Let us take the case study of a person who understands the value of time and considers it no less important than money.

Ravi is the chief executive in a Rs 2,000 crore company. He is the Managing Director at the young age of 35. An MBA from IIM, Ahmedabad, and an engineering graduate from IIT, Delhi, he is a dynamic, young management executive who has climbed fast in his career. With a pay package of Rs1.2 crore, he is leading a healthy, contented life with his family of wife and two children, an eight-year-old boy and a six-year-old-girl. Besides being intelligent, hardworking and efficient in his work, he owes his success to effective time management. This, according to him, is the key to his success and a happy family life. "I do in 24 hours, what others do in 48 hours," says he with a glow in his eyes. Let us see how he manages his time during the week.

Ravi gets up every morning at 5.30. He prepares a cup of tea for himself, not disturbing his wife. After spending half an hour in finishing his morning chores, toilet and shave, he goes in for yoga for half an hour. Then he leaves home for a brisk walk. He is back home around seven, sips another cup of tea along with his wife and goes through the morning newspapers. By eight he is in the bathroom. At half past eight he is eating his breakfast with his wife. He leaves his house at nine.

While being driven to the office, which takes about 45 minutes, Ravi goes through the business newspapers. He marks important news that he would discuss with the relevant departmental heads. Reaching office he spends half an hour with the corporate communication director who updates him with the concerned news in various newspapers. He gives directions on the follow-up with the government departments and discussions to be held with the relevant departments. The follow-up report is to be given to him the following day during meeting. So he remains up-to-date on every matter.

The next meeting is with his personal secretary. She briefs him on the messages and telephones. She also tells him the progress on the previous day directions and orders. He issues necessary instructions, whom to call, what appointments to fix up, and what assignments to complete.

The next two hours are meetings with the different departmental heads. He gets a brief on what has happened 24 hours and how the work is being planned for the next 24 hours. Problems that arose on the previous day and are likely to crop up during the day are also discussed, and the possible line of action is decided. He knows all about delegation. It is, after all, one of the basic tenets of management. So he delegates the works to different departmental heads and forgets those problems for the day.

Till now he has not accepted any call. The secretary knows that he is not to be disturbed unless the call is urgent or from someone very important. Now he is free to talk on the phone. The secretary gives him the list of calls. He indicates the priority and she leaves the room. She has left the mail file. He goes through it while talking on the phone. By the time he has finished with the file and the phones, lunch is ready in the lunch-room. He eats his food with the departmental heads. It is time to discuss the problems in a relaxed manner and settle inter-departmental problems.

Back in his room at two, he is ready to receive visitors. This is also the time when various managers and departmental heads come with problems. Outdoor meetings are also held during this time for which he goes out of the office. He also visits government officers, political leaders and important clients in the afternoon. So he is mostly moving in and out of the office. Afternoons are spent in meetings either in government offices, hotels or in the offices of other companies.

His coming back to the office in not certain. He may come. If he comes, he attends to the business that has emerged during his absence. He uses this time to plan for the coming days.

Normally he leaves office by six in the evening. Back home, he spends time with kids for about an hour. They normally eat their dinner by seven so that they go to the bed by eight. They have to go to school the next morning and so have to get up early.

More often than not, he has to go out for dinner along with his wife. Most of the dinners are office related. Many a time these are social or personal.

But he tries to be back by ten so that he can go to the bed by 11.

The routine is not a fixed one. Being the head of the company he is engaged in various different activities. He goes out of the city and country very often. So he changes his schedule according to the exigencies of work. But one thing is kept in mind—that no time is wasted and every minute is utilised in such a way that he gets the best returns. There is nothing magical about getting the most from the hours available to a person; it is just planning the day and to allot it for various jobs.

Ravi knows the significance of family and never forgets to spend time with the children. Saturdays are exclusively for the children when he takes them for outings and they eat out. He, probably, has taken a leaf out from the book of Sudha Murty. "When my children are at home, I modify my schedule a bit—I spend time with them and their friends, go out for movies etc.," she says in response to the question: "How do you effectively balance the numerous roles in your life?" asked by a correspondent of *Savvy* magazine.

What is the mystery about Ravi's time management? The truth is that there is no mystery. The fact is that Ravi has understood the very fact of life that time is one phenomenon that has been provided equally to every individual, rich or poor. Everyone has 24 hours each day and 168 hours each week to eat, sleep, work, relax, exercise, attend to work, and meetings. There is nothing magical about getting the most from these hours; it is just planning the day and to allot it for various jobs. But time management does require self-discipline and control until the behavioural changes become a part of your functioning system and time management becomes an everyday habit. Plans and schedules for managing time are useless if one does not follow them.

But the secret of Ravi's time management was the *mantra* that he got from Benjamin Franklin, who in 1748 advised a young tradesman: "Remember that time is money."

It made him realise at the beginning of his career that self-discipline and control were essential. He observed both until his behavioural changes were internalised and time management became an essential part of his life. His friends also drew plans and schedules for managing time. But these became useless, as the did not follow them. Essential for effective time management is a sense of balance. Those who are not able to do that and take extreme positions arrive at ridiculous positions. However, it is important to understand the following the time management principles do not ensure the best results. If one entangles oneself in the minutiae details then meaningful tasks would never be accomplished. On the other hand, poor time management skills would not make the person a stooge.

Ravi understood the importance of time management when he went to watch a horse race in Pune. His senior, standing next to him, told him after the race that the winner horse won twice the money than the one that came second. Interestingly, the winner horse did not run twice as fast or went twice as far as the competition to earn twice the money. It only had to be a "nose ahead" of the competition to reap twice the rewards. Time management is much like the horse race metaphor. If one wants to win the race of life, doubling the efforts is not required. The only need is to be a "nose ahead" of others to get better results.

How to be "Nose Ahead" of Others

Five steps were adopted by Ravi to get a "nose ahead." First, every night he *prepared a schedule for the next day* so that there was an action plan to guide him without wasting time on thinking what to do next. He had learnt by experience that whenever he had not done so, he had started the day with the least important work leaving other useful works for the remaining part of the day. At the end of the day he found that many of the listed items were left undone because no time was left for them.

The work schedule for the day contained all the items he wanted to finish during the next day. He prioritised items in order of their importance (#1 for most important, #2 for next most important, etc.), and began the day with the most important item and then went to the next most important item. He followed it up till he reached the end of the schedule. There were days when he could not finish all the items on the list. But that never discouraged him. How much was left undone at the end of the day was not important. What was actually accomplished was all that mattered.

Second, he *planned more than what he thought he would be able to finish* during the day. The Parkinson's Law that stated: "A project tends to take the time allocated for it," was always at the back of his mind. He realised early in the career that planning to finish just one job during the day meant doing that job only. If he decided to finish two jobs during the day he completed both. When he placed six things on the list for the day, he would not get all six done, but he was able to complete three or four items. Planning more than what he could chew created a healthy sense of pressure on Ravi and he naturally became a better time manager. When he had a plateful, he was more focused, suffered less interruptions, and delegated better.

Third, he always *keeps his desk clean* as it creates a better work environment. The saying: "Out of sight; out of mind," is no more relevant for him. What he believes is: "In sight; in mind." An overcrowded desk full of papers and files of all the works he wanted to finish during the day distracted him and pulled him in the wrong direction, accomplishing little of significance.

Fourth, he *does not encourage unnecessary meetings*. He knows that an average business executive spends long hours in meetings. During every business day, hundreds of thousands of meetings are conducted in our country. Studies in developed countries like the United States and the United Kingdom have shown that an average manager spends about 17 hours a week in meetings and about six hours in planning and preparing for those meetings and untold hours in the follow-up. He remembers that as a middle level manager he attended 250 meetings in three months.

Though meetings, where two or more people get together to exchange common information, are an essential part of any business, about as much of a third of the time spent in meetings is wasted due to lack of proper planning and poor meeting management. In fact, most of the meetings are institutional time wasters. Before agreeing to attend any meeting he always asks himself two questions: "Do I contribute anything to that meeting?" and "Do I get anything of value from this meeting?" If the answer to both questions is "No", he tries to find a way to avoid the meeting.

Finally, he *reads a paper only once and takes a decision.* He does not keep it to read it again on some other day and then take a decision. He handles every paper just once. Ravi always avoids the widely followed normal practice of "shuffling blues" when the paper is looked at again and again while the deadline knocks at the doorstep and we get buried under a blizzard of paperwork. When a paper is presented to him, he responds then and there. If it requires serious attention and advice from other persons, he sends it for opinions and schedules it for a time when he will consider it and take a decision.

Time Management Skills

The best results from any operation, whether military or business, can be achieved only when a person acquires certain essential skills. It applies fully on time that must be managed efficiently to get the maximum benefits. Proper time management skills benefit a person in several ways. One, he can plan activities and schedule time for completing them. He can know in advance when he will be busier. He can plan the activities so that those things get done well in time. Two, he can remember meetings, appointments and deadlines so that there are no delays and miss-outs and he becomes more efficient in work.

Time management skills enable the person to implement the work plan in the most effective and efficient way. And the best part is that it does not take much to prepare a plan. For example, a time management plan for a project can be prepared in just less than half a day and the weekly grid in only one hour. It only takes about twenty minutes each week to keep schedules up-to-date, making additions and revisions.

We can continuously improve our time management skills and experience fewer stressful situations resulting from procrastination and/or overextending (trying to do too many activities). It gives us a sense of control over our lives. Let us find out the essential time management skills.

Time management skills are the practical techniques that have helped the highly successful people in business, sports, bureaucracy, politics and public service to reach the pinnacles of their careers. The following time management techniques and strategies are designed to help you manage your time and gain greater control of your life. These should enable you to become a reliable and effective person.

Goal Setting
It is an essential time management skill. One of the factors found common with the successful people

is that they are clear about what they want to achieve. So you must know what you want to get at the end of the day. Without a goal or objective you tend to just drift personally and professionally.

"If you do not know where you are going, it does not matter which road you take," is an oft-repeated saying. And if that is so, you would not know how much time you would take to reach your destination. Without goals, your work would be haphazard, careless and ineffective. A work which should take one hour may take three, or even more, hours.

Goal setting is a useful concept in time management. When you set goals on a routine basis you decide what you want to achieve during the day or the week, or for that matter during a specific time period. Then in a systematic way you move towards the achievement of these goals. The process of setting goals and targets allows you to choose which job to undertake first. By knowing precisely what you want to work, you know what you have to concentrate on to do it. You would also know what might be the distractions.

If you have not set the goal for the day, you would be wandering aimlessly. Sitting at your desk, you would not know how to start your day. A lot of time would be wasted in trying to find out what to do first. Aimlessly, you may start work on any item that catches your eye first. As you are working, you suddenly realise that something else has also to be done. You leave the job at that point and pick up another one. Soon you think of the third one and leave the second and begin the third job. When you walk out of your office at the end of the day, you find that nothing has got finished. Next day would be more confusing, as the previous day's jobs were half done and the current jobs need your time. Having goals around which to focus the day's activities provides the structure for successfully accomplishing them through better time management. Definite goals enable you to have definite control on your time management, and you can accomplish your tasks that are critical for success in your career.

When you are setting goals, always think in terms of specific goals. For instance, when you are planning your day's activities, do not decide that you would read the latest book on marketing that you bought last week from 4 p.m. to 6 p.m. Instead read a definite number of pages of that book in those two hours. Be realistic and fix your goals, keeping in view your capacity and competence.

While setting the goal be practical and a realist in selecting a comfortable time horizon. Fix a goal that can be achieved without much stress. However, do not sulk if because of certain constraints you are not able to achieve your target within a stipulated time period. Try to analyse the reasons for the delay and reallocate the time, more realistically and effectively, next time when you undertake the same work.

Goal setting is a standard technique used by top-level athletes, business people and achievers in all fields. If you also adopt it, it would give you a long-term vision and short-term motivation. It would focus your acquisition of knowledge and help in organising your resources.

Remember not to set modest or small goals. Believe what Mark Victor Hansen said: "Big goals get big results. No goals gets no results or somebody else's results."

Have a Plan

Working according to a plan is another essential time management skill. A plan is like a road map; you need to check it periodically to see if you are still in the right direction. Take time to ask yourself if you are still making progress on your plan. If not, what can you do differently?

A plan is significant because the goals set by you can only be achieved with the help of a well thought out plan. It is a fact that most of the people know what they want to do but hardly a few prepare plans to convert it into reality. They work hard but succeed little, as their activities are not planned.

Planning is nothing but strategic thinking in advance on how you would go ahead in achieving your goal. You have to fix your target and assess the resources you have at your command or you can commission from other sources. Then you have to draw a blueprint of how you will mobilise your resources to go ahead in your work so that the target is achieved within the scheduled timeframe.

Planning is not a one-time job. Plans have to be reviewed and revised regularly. Your yearly plan should be reviewed periodically and reset as your achievements are met. Successful people keep their plans constantly changing. It enables them to stay on top of priorities and remain flexible to changing priorities. This should be done for both personal and business goals.

Plan would enable you to have a place for every work and every work in its place. It would help you to concentrate on one job at one time.

To make an effective and efficient plan, try a four-step strategy:

Identify Immediate Targets You Want to Achieve
Plan every day for the next day. An old saying is: "People do not plan to fail but a lot of people fail to plan." You must spend time each night to take control of the most precious resource you have, the next twenty-four hours. Plan your work and then work according to your plan each day. Prepare a "To Do List" with all you have to do and all you want to do the next day. Without a plan for the

day, you can easily get distracted, spending your time attending to the loudest voice rather than to the most important thing that enhances your productivity.

Select a proper plan that will enable you to complete each target. Dr Eleanor Brantley Schwartz, Chancellor of the University of Missouri, Kansas City, in the United States, accepts that planning enables him to work more. He says: "Time management is central in my life. In order for me to be productive with my jam-packed schedule, I need to plan the slots in which each necessary thing will get done and then see that it gets done within that slot."

Plan Backward

When the plan has been finalised, prepare a backward plan. Start from the deadline goal and move backward, setting deadlines for each segment of the plan till you reach the beginning point. Set dates to each activity. A friend narrated to me how his son, who was sending applications for business schools in the United States, planned backwards to write essays.

Each application required an essay and the deadlines for all the applications were very close together. Initially he thought of writing all the essays in one or two days before the deadlines. But on second thought he realised that the quality of each essay would suffer that may impact the outcome of his applications. So he planned backwards. He fixed dates for different essays. Then he broke each essay into interim goals, such as isolating the main idea and putting it down in writing, doing an outline, writing sections, and completing a first draft. These interim goals were adjusted in his daily work schedules. He was able to write different essays differently and yet devote enough time to his college studies. Not only was he selected for the best business schools, he could afford to see movies and spend time with friends to relax while he was studying and writing essays.

Action Plan
The success of achieving your time-management objective depends on how successfully and effectively you translate your plan into action. An

action plan is a list of tasks that you have to carry out to achieve an objective. It differs from a "To Do List" in that it focuses on the achievement of a single goal.

Wherever you want to do a job, draw up an action plan. This allows you to concentrate on the different stages of the job and monitor your progress towards achieving it.

To draw up an Action Plan, simply list the tasks that you need to carry out to achieve your goal. This is simple, but still very useful. To use it, simply carry out each task in the list.

Try to split the plan into steps that can be easily acted upon.

Important to remember is that your plan depends on your determination, in what you believe in and stand for – your value system. Your values are at the very core of everything you are as a human being and are the unifying principles and core beliefs of your personality and character. The virtues and qualities that you stand for are what constitute the person you have become from the beginning of your life to this moment and is the axle around which the wheel of your life moves.

Know Yourself

As Charles Hamman says: "There are no right or wrong characteristics. The important thing is that you understand what makes you tick so that you can programme yourself more efficiently to take advantage of your strong points and soft-pedal your weaknesses." It is a must to know yourself so that you take advantage of your strong points and favourable factors. You must plan to overcome your shortcomings. Before doing that, ask yourself a few questions: Are you a morning bird or a night worker; task-oriented or people-oriented; an intensive worker or an extensive one; compulsive worker or a deliberative worker?

Are You a Morning Bird or Night Worker

If you are a morning bird, a nine-to-five schedule is the best for you. Such persons wake up refreshed and ready to get into action. The forenoon is highly productive for these people, as they tend to feel tired by the afternoon.

A night worker wakes up slowly and is ready to get going only in the late forenoon. The 9-to-5 schedule is not productive as they are at their top performance by the afternoon. They love to work late in the evening and early night. If you fall into this category, you can easily work up to midnight.

Find out your type and try to know what your prime hours are, and form your day around them. Even if you have to keep your normal office hours, you can schedule your work in such a way that high-priority items are scheduled during your peak hours.

Are You Task-Oriented or People-Oriented?

Task-oriented people love to work on difficult and complex problems and long-term projects. They can remain isolated from others for a long period of time. Such people are most suitable on project designs, developing strategies and financial planning. They may not be their best in marketing and personal relations. On the contrary, people-oriented types are not interested in paperwork or long-term work that keeps them away from action. Such people love to work in a team. They guide and direct other persons to achieve targets. This category of persons excels in marketing and operations.

If you happen to be the former type but have been assigned to work in marketing products, or the latter category person but have been asked to develop a project, don't slug. Schedule these jobs during your peak hours when you are at your best and can exert your greatest discipline and concentration.

Are You an Intensive Person or an Extensive Worker?

The intensive worker cannot work long hours. He can concentrate only for short periods. Such a person should schedule regular breaks to avoid untimely exhaustion. Also he must ensure that, when he starts he takes up the most important job to work upon because he may be left with no energy to do the next job after finishing the first one. The extensive person is slow and steady and needs no breaks during the work. Such people should leave enough time to complete the work without rushing.

Are You Compulsive or Deliberative?

The former is known as A-type worker who enjoys activity and would like to do everything personally. He may not like to delegate power to others and is a workaholic. The latter, known as B-type, works quietly and thrives on his relationships, personal thoughts and feelings.

An A-type will be more effective if he uses his self-control to slow down and does not rush aimlessly from task to task to do everything himself. He should concentrate only on most important activities and leave the low priority jobs to others. The B-type must fix deadlines for each aspect of the work and cut down the amount of paperwork.

Understanding the characteristics and the problems can help you to take steps to avoid the most likely time-management mistakes.

Working by Deadlines

Have a definite deadline. If you do not meet deadlines, take steps to find out why you are unable to do so. Analyse the factors that contributed to your failure. Do not let these mistakes happen again.

The deadlines should be realistic enough to allow for effective performance. Learn to take a decision and deal with the consequences.

Fixing a deadline is an important part of the time management strategy.

A deadline is a commitment that gives a definite shape to any job that you are performing. In the absence of a deadline as a self-imposed pressure point, the work gets postponed and at the end of the day it becomes a rush job. It is of no use because the work completion may become a mere formality and the returns from the work may be minimal. A deadline forces a person to finish the job within the stipulated timeframe. It also helps you to break the job into little bit-sized pieces. Until you quantify your goal, set a deadline, and break it down to its requirements, the resolution will forever remain unattainable. The deadline will make the work a part of your open file that you cannot ignore or shuffle it off. It can help you in developing a time-management perspective in three ways.

One, it divides the work into segments and assigns deadlines to each segment. Just one deadline may give you an incentive for completion, but it may not help you in finishing the different segments of the job in time. Remember that the job is not done at one go. It has to be divided into different segments and each segment is to be completed on time.

Two, while fixing the deadlines keep in view your credibility of finishing the work on time. There are people who always finish work on time while others are still struggling when the deadline is over. Those who work in daily newspapers develop this habit. If you find that you have been a failure in meeting the deadline, try to find out reasons for that. If you are serious and remove the reasons for not maintaining deadlines, finishing work on deadline will be a normal routine.

Three, reward successes and punish failures. When you and your team finish the work on time have a ball, party or celebration. Such activity boosts the moral of the group and establishes your leadership. The team develops a faith and respect in you. Next time you would get a better cooperation and may be able to finish the work before the deadline. Whenever you miss the deadline, analyse the factors and see that they are not repeated in future.

Remember that a deadline acts as a "forcing system" in your subconscious mind. It motivates you to do the things necessary to make your goal come true. If it is a big goal, set sub-deadlines as well. Don't leave this to chance.

Improve Your Time Management

Everyone is given the same amount of time—24 hours a day and seven days in a week. And if you multiply that out you have a total of 168 hours a week. And the unique thing about time is that it can only be spent, it cannot be saved. But different people spend it in different ways, some intelligently, some foolishly. Most of us are at wit's end wondering how to get everything done and still have a life, how we can finish more work in less time and spend good time with the family. We suggest five techniques to help you to get at least one more hour out of your productive day.

1. Maintain Balance

The life of a person can be divided into seven areas: health, family, financial, intellectual, social, professional, and spiritual. Normally a person does not spend equal amount of time in each area. But, if, in the long run, the person is spending a sufficient quantity and quality of time in each area, then his life is balanced. In case the balance is not maintained, will spend more time in another area. It will be waste of time that could have been saved if that area were not ignored in the past. When you do not spend enough time to take care of your body and health, you will waste a lot of your time when you fall sick. If you have been ignoring your family, you will realise the mistake later and may have to spend a lot more time to re-establish relationships. So you should maintain a healthy balance between the various areas of life through efficient time management.

2. Write Things Down

Then pen can provide better memory than the keenest mind. Develop the habit of jotting down all the works you want to do during they day or in the following days. Our mind is a unique machine. It is good for the overall picture but fails to record small and minor details. The details, in fact, are more important that can be managed with the pen. Writing things down helps you to more easily remember all that you need to accomplish.

3. Plan the Day

It is said that people do not plan to fulfil but a lot of people fail to plan. Train yourself to take control, every night, of the most precious resource at your command, the next 24 hours. Plan your work and then work your plan each day. Prepare a 'To Do List' (TDL) which should include all the works you want to do the next day. Without a TDL you can easily get distracted; spending your time on least important things rather then the most important things.

Look at the TDL before you start your day. Keep the plan on your desk or pin it on the wall in front of you or paste it on the dashboard of your car. Score your performance at the end of the day.

4. Prioritise

Effective time management demands developing a time strategy that should be based on a short list of time priorities.

Identify the task that you think is the most important for you in your work and the time you must devote to complete it; then the number two and then the number three; etc. This short list of time priorities should form the foundation for your time planning for every week of the year. If you have not done that you will not be able to decide what is the most important task for you to start the day. You would end up in a crisis situation, as all tasks would get stalled. You would involve yourself in managing the crisis rather doing the normal work. Sudha Murty has never faced a crisis situation as she always prioritises her office work and starts with the most urgent and important task on hand.

Remember what Jim Rohn said: "We can no more afford to spend major time on minor things than we can to spend minor time on major things," Assign time according to the priority of the job.

5. Control Procrastination

Procrastination is a worldwide phenomenon. Most of us procrastinate and put off important things because we are unable to assess the damages of delayed action. To get going on something you have been putting off, create in your mind enough pain for the damage caused for not doing it or enough pleasure to do it. The pleasure approach is better. You can do so by turning the procrastinated project into a game, working with one thing at a time so other things do not distract you. Break it down to small, manageable pieces. Get it started, take the first step and you will likely continue it to completion.

You can improve the quantity and quality of your work with the help of a sprinting concept. Select a few days in a row. Start early and work late at full speed. After three-four days of sprinting, return to your normal schedule. It would definitely become faster and more efficient than before. Whenever you feel that your capacity is beginning to drop, schedule a sprinting session again.

Time Management Tips
 Scheduling and managing time wisely should be the two important aspects of the work culture of a modern day successful person. Missing important

appointments and deadlines cause complications to both your business and family lives, resulting in, more often than not, anxiety, frustration, guilt, and other nasty feelings. These may cause immense monetary and emotional loss to you. Therefore, it is necessary that you should make the most of your time. Let us see how you can do it.

The first thing, if you want to manage your time, is to have a clear idea of how your day is divided between the routine and business activities. A personal time survey is needed to help you to understand how much of your time is spent on routine activities and what amount of time is left for work and business. To get a more accurate estimate, you should keep track of how much time you spend in a week on your routine activities. It will also help you identify your time wasters. Here we give you an example of how you can conduct a survey to find out how you are spending time on various activities during your 24 hours. In money management, people are encouraged to keep a financial diary to get an idea where their money goes. You can't change spending patterns until you know what they are! The same holds true for time. Do you ever find yourself saying something like, "Where did all the time go?" If we want to change how we use time to be more in line with our priorities, the first step is tracking how we spend it. Ideally, you would track your time spending habits for a week. Identify how you spend your time in areas such as time for self, family, friends, job, household work, church/community activities and sleep. Then identify how you would like to spend your time and list any changes you would like to make.

The following schedule shows the various routine activities you normally perform during a day. When working on the survey, estimate the amount of time you spend every day on each activity and multiply it by seven. This will give you the total time spent on the activity in one week. After each item's weekly time has been calculated, add all these times for the grand total. Subtract this from 168, the total possible hours per week.

1. Number of hours of sleep each night   x 7 =
2. Number of grooming hours per day   x 7 =
3. Number of hours for meals/snacks per day
   (include preparation time)   x 7 =
4a. Total travel time weekdays   x 5 =
4b. Total travel time weekends   x 2 =
5. Number of hours per week for regularly
   performed functions (clubs, get-togethers, etc.)
6. Number of hours per day for chores, errands,
   extra grooming, etc.   x 7 =
7. Number of average hours per week socialising,
   dates, etc.   Total:

   Subtract the above number from   168 =

The remaining hours are the hours you have available for work.

Now you should plan how your time should be managed. The following chapters should help you in planning and doing that.

Time Wasters

An efficient time management process ensures that you do not waste any time on non-productive activities. It becomes necessary, therefore, to know what aspects of your work and personal life lead to wastage of time. Here are the most frequent factors that lead to inefficient and ineffective time management. These are known as *Time Wasters*.

You may frequently find it difficult to implement your best plans or intentions. For that these time-wasters are the culprits. Therefore, safeguarding your time is essential. You need to protect your time by saying "no" to various time-wasting interruptions, activities, requests, or persons. Though it is difficult, fortunately there are strategies you can use to reduce, if not eliminate, time wastage and, be more in control of the situation and reduce stress. But before that you must know what damages your time management efficiency. Here we mention a number of time wasters:

Interruption

Like everything, interruptions that are nothing more than "unanticipated events" are both good and bad. We all work on a daily basis for "good" interruptions, those that are "crucial" and "important". In fact, we welcome and are paid for to handle those "good" interruptions. Those are not to be considered time wasters. What affects our higher levels of productivity are the "bad" interruptions, those that add "little" or "no" value to our work output.

One example of "good" interruption is when a customer drops in at your office to place an order. Another example is your colleague interrupting you to show how to complete the delayed project in less time. These are all interruptions but they will lead to enhanced results. So, they are very good.

Examples of "bad" interruptions are when your boss drops in to tell that he would like to play golf with you this weekend, though it is four days away, or a salesman telephones you at work and tries to sell something that you do not need or want.

In India we do not take work interruptions seriously and, therefore, not much work has been done to assess it. However, a number of studies have been conducted in the United States on work interruptions. Here are some interesting statistics:

An average American experiences one interruption every 8 minutes or approximately 6-7 per hour. In an eight-hour day, that totals around 50-60 interruptions in the day. The average interruption takes approximately 5 minutes. (Some may take several hours or days; others may only take a few seconds.) If he is receiving 50 interruptions in the day and each takes 5 minutes, that adds up to 250 minutes or just over 4 hours, then 50 per cent of an eight-hour working day must be a waste.

Interruption is a twofold problem: the interruption itself, and the expectation of further interruption. Both reduce your efficiency considerably. Constant interruptions kill any hope of effective time management. So find ways to check them. Some interruptions can be avoided by keeping in mind the following:

Arrange your work area in such a way that the disturbing elements are at your back. These may be a window or a glass panel through which you can see the whole office. Fix your chair, if it can be done, in such a way that you do not see the flow of the traffic or the people working in the office.

Close your door; open it selectively. Make it clear that when your door is closed you are not to be disturbed. An open door policy is good only for those who want to keep a watch on their office staff. Usually a supervisory officer would do that. If you have a responsible position and have to do a lot of conceptual work or serious reading of files, keep the door closed. You will be able to do more and better work.

If you do not have a separate room or cabin and have to concentrate on some important work, find and use a special space such as a library carrel or an office where friends will be unable to find you.

Have regular meetings, maybe every week, with the people that you interact with the most, and insist on saving non-pressing issues for these meetings.

Telephone

The facility is the greatest invention for better time management. However, paradoxically this is also biggest enemy to time management. It usually is because people keep on calling all times. During the day a large number of calls may not be of any importance to work. Callers have also the tendency of prolonging conversation and reducing your work time. I have often gone to the office of chief executive officers and in thirty minutes of stay I was able to talk to him for less than five minutes. The problem was not just the time that the interruption itself consumed, but the time he needed to catch up mentally to where he was before he was interrupted. Therefore, to have better time management you should know how to control its hold over you.

Most of us would not agree that a lot of time is wasted on telephone. To understand time wastage on phone it is suggested a time log be maintained for a few days. It will show how much time telephone interruptions take away from your working day. Then try various methods to reduce time wastage on telephone.

Return telephone calls when it is more convenient for you. Do not hold on for long. Instead, agree on a time to ring back or leave a message and your phone number. If someone is unavailable find out the best time to call back, or leave your number.

If you need to make regular calls agree upon a mutually beneficial time.

Learn to leave clear messages on other people's answering machines. Always leave your name and phone number if you want them to ring you back.

Train your personal secretary or a member of your personal staff to screen calls and refer them to others. The PA should politely tell your time constraints to the caller.

Always keep a pen and pad by the phone.

If you get a call asking for information you don't have immediate access, do not look for it; arrange to call back later. Plan your telephone calls. Make a brief note of what you want to say and find out. If you have several phone calls to make, do them all in a cluster.

Do not keep on talking endlessly. Set a time limit for each call. A three-minute egg-timer, that was widely used in olden days for trunk calls, seems the best devise to monitor time. Though archaic, it serves the purpose very nicely even today.

Lack of Priorities
This probably is the biggest and the most important time waster as it affects all the work we do, both professionally and personally. Those who accomplish the most in a day know exactly what they want to accomplish. Unfortunately many of us think that goals and objectives are a yearly phenomenon and not daily considerations. This results in too much time being spent on the minor things and not on the things which are important to our work and lives.

Prioritising your responsibilities and engagements is very important. Some people do not know how to prioritise and, consequently, become procrastinators.

Attempting Too Much
Many people feel that they have to accomplish everything in a single day and don't give themselves enough time to do things properly. This leads only to half-finished projects with no feeling of achievement.

You must not be over ambitious, and should control your ambitions to fit your abilities and situation. Ask yourself what exactly you want to prove. Be realistic by maintaining a perception. Do not kill yourself. Recognise that if you unrealistically attempt too much, you may not achieve anything. Determine what in reality you want to achieve, focus on that, and learn to live with the fact that you may have regrets, no matter what.

Unexpected Visitors
How often you hear the five deadliest words that rob your time: "Have you got a minute?" Everyone

can be a culprit—colleagues, the boss, and your peers. Knowing how to deal with such people is one of the best skills you can learn. Distinguish between being available for business and for socialising. Go to the office of others before they come to yours. Meet them outside your room. Move up to the door to receive the person and keep talking to him rather than asking him to come in and have a seat. Preset your time limit on each visit.

If you have an unexpected visitor, try to find out at the very beginning why he has come. Stand up and move towards him when he enters the room, so that he also remains standing. If it is necessary for you to deal personally with him suggest a later meeting, at your convenience. If possible, suggest a meeting in his office. Set time limits to your discussion. Avoid engaging in small talk. If you have a secretary or PA, agree upon a clear policy about who can have access to you and whom they should deal with.

Ineffective Delegation
Trying to do everything yourself means attending to insignificant works too. It means wasting a good

amount of time on minor tasks which can be attended to by your juniors. Good delegation is a key skill in both managers and leaders to do more in less time. The best managers have an ability to delegate work to their staff and ensure that it is performed correctly. This, probably, is the best way of building a team's moral and reducing your workload at the same time. The general rule is if one of your staff can do 80 per cent of the work as well as you can, then delegate it.

The Cluttered Desk

An unorganised desk is a common sight in offices and is a major reason of time wastage. If your desk is full of papers and files, how do you decide what to do and from where to get the information? One managing director of a successful company was asked why he had only one file on his desk. His reply was that he can concentrate on only one item at a time and that he was far more effective if he worked that way. So when you begin your day look at your desk. If you can see less than 80 per cent of it then you are probably suffering from 'desk stress'. The most effective people work from clear desks.

You must impose strict order on your workspace—a place for everything and everything in its place, with neat files, a clean desktop, a floor you can actually walk on.

Procrastination

Delaying or putting off action is the biggest thief of time. Decision avoidance is more harmful than no-decision making. By reducing the amount of procrastination you can substantially increase the amount of active time available to you for working your tasks.

One of the best ways for you to overcome procrastination and get more things done faster is for you to have everything you need at hand before you begin. When you are fully prepared, you are like a fully loaded gun. You just need one small mental push to get started on your highest value tasks.

Some other time-wasters are boredom, too many ideas, and lack of confidence, overconfidence, thoughtlessness and indecisiveness.

One of the classic rules of time management is not to work for everyone uniformly. You have to find your own way through the suggestions and exercise that follow. However, it may not be possible to control some elements of your life and works you want to do.

Tips for Saving Time

Now that you know how you spend most of your time and what the major time-wasters are, think about what your most important tasks are. Do you have enough time to complete all of them in your timeframe? The chances are that you are always short of time. Below are some tips on how to schedule and budget your time when it seems you just don't have enough.

Planing and Organising Your Work
The time spent in thinking and planning is never a waste. It is time well spent. In fact, if you fail to take time for planning, you are, in effect, planning to fail. Organise your schedule in a way that makes sense to you. Much on it has been written in an earlier chapter.

Learning to Say 'No' When You Can

It is a normal human nature to dump the work or problems on to the shoulders of others. Your colleague enters your room and wants you to take care of the tender document because he was having a headache. You are already behind your schedule and are struggling to finish your file. But like most other people you lack the skill to just say 'no' for fear of upsetting your colleague. On some other day, an old friend of yours drops in at the office and wants to take you to a cricket match. You have important works to complete. But you do not want to annoy your friend. You go with him and suffer as the deadlines were disturbed. Though a small word of two letters, most of us find it difficult to utter it. If one can develop the habit of politely saying 'no' when deadlines are closeby, time management will be more effective. You would be able to do more work as saying 'no' frees up time for the things that are most important.

However, it does not mean that you should always say 'no' to every request from friends and relatives. One has to be discreet in selecting the request to say 'no'. Here are some guidelines:

Thoughtless and inappropriate requests can always be turned down. If someone asks you to drop him at the railway station that is 40 kilometres away, when regular buses or inexpensive taxis are available, you can understand the request to be thoughtless. On the other hand, if you are being requested to take someone seriously ill to the hospital, it would be inhuman to say 'no'.

You should say 'no', if the request made to you conflicts with your own priorities. Also, you should be careful not to commit others against your will. If your friend asks you to bring the whole family for dinner, you should say 'no' if you have to finish important office files or prepare a note for presentation.

Now comes the most important aspect of the whole situation—how to say 'no'?

It must be said promptly. If you delay or postpone, unnecessary hopes would be raised. If someone asks you to help his son in doing his homework, it would be tempting to delay saying 'no' so as to soften the blow of refusal. But this may create some sour feelings. It would be better to politely say sorry, that you were occupied for the time being, and that you would definitely help him when you would be free.

It is not necessary to justify every 'no'. You have a right to take a decision keeping in view your own priorities or requirements. This is particularly true when people make unreasonable demands.

Refusal must be firm, yet uttered without any expression of impatience and anger. If you softly express your inability, you would find that your refusal has been taken well. You should always decline with serenity and assurance.

Get used to asking yourself, 'Am I the right person for this job?' If you think you are not, say 'no'.

Having a "To Do List (TDL)"

Write down the tasks that you have to perform during the day. If they are large, break them down into their component elements. If these still seem large, break them down again. Do this until you have listed everything that you have to do. It can be prepared either the last thing the previous day or the first thing in the morning. "When I go for my morning walks, I make a list of things-to-do-today," says Sudha Murty, wife of N R Narayan Murty.

The TDL is a list of all jobs that you want to finish during the day. It consolidates all the jobs that you have to do into one place. TDL is essential where you need to carry out a number of different sorts of tasks, or where you have made a number of commitments. If you find that you are often caught out because you have forgotten to do something, then you need to keep a 'To Do List'. Though TDLs are very simple, they are extremely powerful, both as a method of organising yourself and as a way of reducing stress. Often problems may seem overwhelming or you may have a seemingly huge number of demands on your time. This may leave you feeling out of control, and overburdened with work.

TDL should be prioritised so that those things that are important and add the greatest value to your work are attended first and other less important later. Assign importance to each task and mark the importance of the task next to it. Write '1' against the most important task and '5' to the least important ones. If too many tasks have a high priority, run through the list again and downgrade the less important ones. Once you have done this, rewrite the list in priority order. Rewrite the list according to the assigned order of importance. It will be your precise plan that you can use to eliminate the problems you face when you forget certain tasks. You will be able to take care of them in order of importance. This would allow you to separate important jobs from the many time-consuming trivial ones. Now carry out the jobs at the top of the list first. These are the most important, most beneficial tasks to complete.

Different people can use TDLs in different ways. Those in the sales department should keep the list relatively short and aim to complete it every day. It would be a good way of motivating you. In an operational role, or where the tasks are large or you have to be dependent on too many other people, it may be better to keep one list and 'chip away' at it. It may be that you carry unimportant jobs from one TDL to the next. Your worry may be that you may not be able to complete some very low priority jobs for several months. One way to deal with such situations, if you are running up against a deadline for them, is to raise their priority.

Though TDLs are very simple, they are extremely powerful, both as a method of organising yourself and as a way of reducing stress. Often problems may seem overwhelming or you may have a seemingly huge number of demands on your time. This may leave you feeling out of control, and overburdened with work. TDLs are fundamentally important for effective and efficient working. If you use TDLs, you will ensure that you remember to carry out all necessary tasks; that you tackle the most important jobs first, and do not waste time on trivial tasks; you do not get stressed by large volumes of unimportant jobs.

Finding Time for Unfinished Jobs

Time needs to be managed because we don't have enough time to do everything that we want and need to do. In particular, we never seem able to "find time" for those important but not urgent activities.

Stop finding excuses for lack of time. You'll never find time if you develop a negative attitude. Decide that you will have to find time, one way or the other, to finish the incomplete jobs by better time management. Look towards people who are doing more work than you in the same span of time. You have to consciously decide to work in their ways and not others. You have to make time by taking it away from one activity and giving it to another.

Conscientious and creative use of the to-do list can help here. If you want to exercise three times a week, if you need to do some long-range career and financial planning, if you care enough about another human being to want to nurture your relationship, you will schedule time for these things. Otherwise, you may not "get to them", and even if you do, you'll give them only your leftover time, when energy and focus are at the lowest.

You can have more time for many important things in life by reducing time spent on the items in the last category, the "neither important nor urgent but just a lot of fun" area. But you shouldn't ignore this area completely (even if you could). If you do that your life will become very uninteresting, like an appointment with the doctor. A friend of mine, often working on two crossword puzzles a day, used to justify it saying that he, after all, was a journalist. "Words are my tools (as well as one of my passions). Crossword puzzles expand my vocabulary," he would say. However, I do not try to justify crossword puzzles that way. I solve them because they're fun for me. That's enough. But when I need to make time for something else, I can cut them out.

You can also create time for yourself by slicing some of that "urgent but not important or even a lick of fun" stuff out.

Combining Several Activities

Another suggestion is to combine several activities into one time spot. While commuting to work, listen to taped notes. This allows up to an hour or two a day of good work review. While taking a shower make a mental list of the things that need to be done. When you watch a TV serial, laugh as you look into your files. Mrs Indira Gandhi, the former Prime Minister of India, used to go through her office files while watching the TV. These are just suggestions of what you can do to combine your time, but there are many others. Above all, be creative and let it work for you. Sudha Murty indulges in a lot of parallel processing, for example, "As I am talking over the phone, I instruct my assistant or do some other work of my own, or I catch up with friends on the phone while I am cooking," she says.

Do not be Rigid

Even the most perfect people cannot follow their time-schedules very rigidly. You must allow time for some degree of interruptions and distractions. It is better to plan for 75 per cent of your time so that you will have the flexibility to handle interruptions and the unplanned "emergencies".

Using Prime Time Effectively

At a particular period of the day, when you are at your best, involve in the most important and serious work. Knowing when your best time is and planning to use that time of the day for your priorities are effective time management.

Doing the Right Thing Right

Noted management expert, Peter Drucker, says "Doing the right thing is more important than doing things right." Doing the right thing is effectiveness; doing things right is efficiency. Focus first on effectiveness (identifying what is the right thing to do), then concentrate on efficiency (doing it right).

Avoiding Emergencies

It is not good to let emergencies develop. Such situations usually develop when timely actions are not taken to solve routine matters. Emergencies have short-term consequences while important tasks are those with long-term, goal-related implications. If you reduce emergencies you'll have all the time for all your important priorities. If you find ways to handle important matters well in time, they may not become emergencies. The best way to avoid emergencies is to plan ahead so that you can anticipate some problems and solve them in advance.

Organising Papers

Allowing papers to accumulate on your desk and your office is an indication of inefficiency and time waste. Devise ways to screen your papers more effectively. You should get your mail screened by your secretary. S/he should be trained to sift the unnecessary mail from the important one. Only the latter should be presented to you. The former can be answered by him/her and filed. If someone else can reply any mail, it should be forwarded to that person. Do not waste time in reading full reports. Look for the summary or someone should prepare an executive summary for you. Read those parts of the report which are important or need decision by you.

A good follow-up system saves time in more ways than one.

Managing Information

Not getting information when you need it leads to frustration and a lot of time wastage. The best way to guarantee that you'll have the needed information when you need it is to organise your needs systematically. Organise the information you have in your office in a systematic way in different files. Also, have the list of sources from where you can collect information when needed. Obtaining information from others, especially those outside your system, requires tact, diplomacy, and resourcefulness. When you are requesting for information, you must describe fully what you need, and when. Unless it is confidential and strategic, also explain why you need the information.

Self-discipline

If you want most of your time management techniques to work you must be disciplined. Being disciplined means sticking with one important job until it is finished. It needs a strong discipline to attend to important office job when friends and colleagues are enjoying a cricket match or weekend picnic. It takes discipline to refrain from interrupting a co-worker to ask about a routine matter.

One cause of weak self-discipline is poor health or even simple fatigue. If you are not feeling well, you always don't have the mental and emotional energy to concentrate on the job at hand. Take care of yourself. Indulge in a regular exercise programme. Review what you eat and drink. Avoid junk foods, excessive smoking and alcohol. Get some extra sleep. Take a mini-vacation with your family during the weekend. Go to a natural resort or a hill station or the sea beach.

Another cause of this problem is lack of interest in the work. It may be that you do not like the assignment that has been given to you. If there is no way of changing it, develop a positive attitude toward your work and develop a feeling of accomplishment. It will energise you and provide a boost that you need to recover enthusiasm about work.

Self-discipline is a part of the personality, and lack of it is a habit. Ask yourself a question: "Do I want to see myself as a failed person?"

One time-tested solution to self-discipline is autosuggestion and self-talk. If you tell yourself over and over again that you are an organised person and that you have the discipline to do what is to be done, many problems related with a weak discipline will be avoided.

Disciplined people have common characteristics. They do not settle for "almost", and they do not give up. They set tough targets for themselves and keep going until they reach them. Then they set even higher goals.

Focusing on Importance

The secret of time management is to concentrate on results, not on being busy. Get focused and believe in what is neatly summed up in the Pareto Principle, or the "80:20 Rule". It states that typically 80 per cent of unfocused effort generates only 20 per cent of results. The remaining 80 per cent of results are achieved with only 20 per cent of the effort. True, the ratio may not always be 80:20, however, this broad pattern of a small proportion of activity generating more than proportionate returns is very true. It happens so frequently as to be the norm in many areas. Most of us spend a large part of our time in a frenzy of activity, but achieve very little because we are not concentrating on the right things. You must learn to focus on tasks that are the most important, leaving the less important ones for your juniors. Remember that you are hired to do the most difficult jobs and not all the ones. Do not try to do everything yourself. Concentrate on works those no one else can do.

If you busy yourself with trivial tasks or those tasks which give low value returns you neglect high productive tasks.

To be a better-focused person you should calculate the cost of your time. This helps you to find out if you are spending your time profitably. If you work for an organisation, calculate how much you cost it each year. Include your salary, the cost of office space you occupy, equipment and facilities you use, expenses, administrative support, etc. If you are self-employed, work the annual running costs of your business. To this figure add an amount of profit you should generate by your activity.

If you work normal hours, you will have approximately 200 productive days each year. If you work 7½ hours each day, this equates to 1,500 hours in a year.

From these figures, calculate an hourly rate. This should give a reasonable estimate of how much your time is worth— this may be a surprisingly large amount!

When you are deciding whether or not to take a task on, think about this value—are you wasting your or your organisation's resources on a low yield task?

Calculating how much your time is worth helps you to work out whether it is worth doing particular jobs. An important part of focusing on results is working out what to focus on! Many people work very hard all day doing little jobs that do not actually affect the quality of their work.

To get focused, you must ask yourself this question continually: "What can I, and only I, do that, if done well, will make a real difference?"

Peter Drucker, the management guru, suggested this question. It is one of the best questions for achieving personal effectiveness. What can you, and only you, do those, if done well, can make a real difference?

This is something that only you can do. If you don't do it, someone else won't do it. But if you do it, and you do it well, it can really make a difference to your life and your career. What is your answer to this question?

Every hour of every day, you can ask yourself this question and there will be a specific answer. Your job is to be clear about the answer and then to start and work on this task before anything else.

Travel

Business means travel and if the position is important, it may be extensive—domestic as well as foreign. It can be a great waste of time if travel is not managed properly. However, if you are well organised, travel can be a major time-saver. It gives you uninterrupted work time. There are no phone calls, no casual visitors, no meetings, and if there is a crisis, someone else takes care of it. In two hours of flight time, you can accomplish what would take you three hours of normal time in the office. If that is to be achieved, travel has to be planned and managed well to get the maximum out of it. The entire travel should be organised in such a way that you get the most out of your time from the moment you leave until you return. If you have layovers, put that time to effective use. Schedule appointments at airport, make phone calls or do some reading.

Carefully plan the papers you would need during the tour. You cannot make decisions on matters unless you have the necessary background files with you. Be sure to include all the things you may need: writing materials, calculator, dictating machine and laptop computer. Do not forget extra batteries and the phone cord for uploading material to your assistant's computer.

Prepare a detailed appointment schedule with names, addresses, and phone numbers of all business contacts, including residential numbers. Dates, times, and places of appointments should be listed along with any pertinent instructions on locating the addresses.

Don't waste time in making the travel arrangements yourself. Leave it to a professional travel agent. After your appointments are confirmed, have the flights booked accordingly. Avoid arriving or departing during the local rush hour.

If you travel frequently, make a checklist of personal items for both cold and warm weather destinations. Try wherever possible to restrict your luggage to a carry bag; you will not waste time on waiting for the baggage on your arrival.

Before you leave, discuss how the work would be organised during your absence. Discuss possible problems that may arise when you are away. The office persons should know the extent of their authority during your absence. They should know which decisions they can take and which should wait for your return.

Make arrangements to phone the office at a set time every day.

Travel only when it is a must. Look at all the other ways of accomplishing your travel mission. See if the other party can be invited to come to see you. You can send someone else or use other communication methods.

If you travel every day to work by train, bus or car, you can put that time to good use. Various alternatives available are: business readings, writing reports or replying to the correspondence. The mobile is a great time saver.

Do Not be a Perfectionist
Nobody can be perfect. In the Malaysian culture, only the gods are capable of producing anything perfect. Whenever something is made, a flaw is left on purpose so the gods do not feel offended. If you try to be a perfect person, be prepared for defeat. Difficult tasks usually result in avoidance and procrastination. You need to set achievable goals, but they should also be challenging. There will always be people both weaker and stronger than you. True, some things need to be closer to perfection than others are, but perfectionism, paying unnecessary attention to detail, can be a

form of procrastination. Learn to accept reasonable, adequate work.

Rewarding Yourself
Even for small successes, celebrate achievement of goals. Promise yourself a reward for completing each task, or finishing the total job. Then keep your promise to yourself and indulge in your reward. Doing so will help you maintain the necessary balance in life between work and play. As Ann McGee-Cooper says, "If we learn to balance excellence in work with excellence in play, fun, and relaxation, our lives become happier, healthier, and a great deal more creative."

People who use these techniques routinely are the highest achievers in all walks of life, from business to sport to public service. If you use these skills well, you will be able to function effectively even under intense pressure. Rewards help you to get the most out of the limited time you have.

Concentration
Increase your work capacity by concentrating more effectively. Adopt the four-step formula of

increasing your concentration. Prepare yourself for the work; concentrate on a task until you reach a logical or natural break; try your mind for action by reading or discussing the basics of the task until you understand it thoroughly; and, keep a record of your performance at various intervals.

Clearing Your Desk

Begin by clearing off your desk or workspace so that you only have one task in front of you. If necessary, put everything on the floor or on the table behind you. Gather all the information, reports, details, papers, and work materials that you will require for completing the job. Have them at hand so you can reach them without getting up or moving. Be sure that you have all writing materials, computer discs, access codes, e-mail addresses and everything else you need to start and continue working until the job is done.

Work Area

Set up your work area so that it is comfortable, attractive and conducive to working for long periods. Especially make sure that you have a comfortable chair that supports your back and allows your feet to sit flat on the floor.

The most productive people take the time to create a work area where they enjoy spending time. The cleaner and neater your work area before you begin, the easier it is for you to get started and keep going.

Sprinting
Improve the quantity and quality of your work with the help of the sprinting concept. Select a few days in a row. Start early and work late at full speed. After three-four days of sprinting, return to your normal schedule. It would definitely become faster and more efficient than before. Whenever you feel your capacity beginning to drop, schedule a sprinting session again.

Lastly, take a small chunk of the job and do it right away. Decide quickly whether or not you can do it. If you can't do it, drop it immediately, However, do not drop everything.

By applying the skills in this chapter you can optimise your efforts to ensure that you concentrate as much of your time and energy as possible on the high payoff tasks. This ensures that you achieve the greatest benefit possible with the limited amount of time available to you.

Success in business requires wise management of four kinds of resources: human, work, information and time. All the first three can be manipulated in many directions. Human resources can be managed in several ways. You can increase or decrease the number of persons working for you; you can change the composition of your work force—adding more of a certain speciality and reducing others; you can shift workers from one department to another. In the the same way work and information can be manipulated, modified and changed in various combinations. Time is the only resource that is unique.

Time, the invisible resource, is unique, because it is finite. There are only 24 hours in a day, and no matter what you do, you cannot increase the number. The clock cannot be fastened or slowed down. Time is the only resource that must be spent the moment it is received, and it must be spent at one fixed rate: sixty seconds per minute, sixty minutes per hour. So we cannot control the amount of time we have, we can only manage its usage. We cannot choose whether or not to spend it; we can only think how to use it. Once we have not used it, it is wasted, it is gone forever—and cannot be replaced. In the earlier chapters we have made an effort to suggest how you should manage yourself in relation to time, because you cannot manage time.

Time management (or self management) is not a hard subject to understand. It is important to build time management techniques into your daily routine. If you do not do that you'll only achieve partial (or no) results and then make comments, such as, "I tried time management once and it doesn't work for me." Significant to remember is that the more time we spend planning our time and activities the more time we will have for those activities. By fixing goals and eliminating time-wasters every day you will have extra time in the week to spend on leisure with family.

Remember time management is the core skill for success. Your ability to manage your time, to focus and channel your energies on your highest-value tasks, will determine your rewards and your level of accomplishment in life more than any other factor. With good time management you can save yourself a minimum of two hours a day. You can, with the help of these two hours, have more time with your family and avoid getting stressed out. You would have a better quality of life. Also you can improve your productivity and be more successful in achieving your goals. It would give you more professional satisfaction and rewards.

In the final analysis, nothing will help you more in your career than to get the reputation as a person who gets important work done quickly and in the best way. This reputation will make you one of the most valuable and respected people in your field. Only effective and efficient time management will ensure that.

Check Your Time Management Efficiency Quotient (TMEQ)

Do you manage your time effectively and efficiently? Rank yourself on the five-point scale following the clues mentioned below. To find out any improvement, do it again three months from now. Honestly give ranking to each question and find out your TMEQ with the help of the score table to find out your TMEQ with the help of the score table at the end of the chapter.

Crisis Management

(1) I always anticipate things that are likely to go wrong and take proper steps to prevent them and if they happen, to mitigate their consequences.

(2) I demand reports from my staff on all jobs that they are asked to handle and identify problems and take corrective steps.

(3) After fixing goals, I discuss all alternatives for achieving them and select those which are not likely to generate crisis.

(4) If crises emerge, I do not commit more resources than essential and immediately decide on the suitable steps and individuals who would carry out my decisions.

(5) When the crisis is over, I call the meeting of all team members for a post-analysis. Also to suggest what steps should be taken if a similar situation arises in future. Suitable steps are implemented immediately.

Telephone Interruptions

(1) My secretary screens all telephone calls carefully.

(2) I limit my conversations on telephone by a three-minute egg-timer, or a reminder from my PA.

(3) Before accepting a phone call, I find out its purpose so that I determine its relative priority.

(4) Before proceeding with a call, I find out who else might be equally or better situated to talk to the person calling, or whether the call can be postponed in everyone's best interest.

(5) I use a mechanical answering device when I do not want to be disturbed.

Planning
(1) I am clear about the objectives, priorities and plans of my company.
(2) I translate these objectives into monthly, weekly and daily goals.
(3) I keep these goals visible and measure my progress against them.
(4) When two priorities are conflicting with each other, I consider what is more important for that day and give precedence to that priority.
(5) All priorities are agreed upon, understood and communicated by my entire team.

Overloading
(1) When I feel that any of my staff members is feeling overloaded with work, I find out how effectively he is working.
(2) I do not accept low-value or inappropriate requests.
(3) I look for the inability to say "no" to the boss and practise the various techniques for asserting myself when appropriate.

(4) I fix reasonable time limits to various jobs.

(5) When facing overload situations, I try to find out how the person is organising the work and take steps to improve working systems.

Unannounced Visitors

(1) Any unannounced visitor is screened effectively.

(2) I always complete the task in hand before permitting an interruption.

(3) I time-limit interruptions whenever possible through my secretary, or myself if I do not have that kind of assistance.

(4) Before accepting an interruption, I always ask what it is about so that I can assess its priority.

(5) Before processing with an interruption, I try to find out: What efforts have been done to solve the problem? Who else might be equally or better equipped to help? Could a postponement be in everyone's best interests? What would happen if nothing were done?

Delegating Work

(1) I find out, before assigning the job, whether or not the person is suitable.

(2) I accept that the best way to train a person is to assign him a job that he has not done earlier.

(3) I provide direction and keep control on the person to increase his motivation level.

(4) If someone indulges in reverse delegation, I refuse to permit it.

(5) I demand regular progress reports on all major delegated tasks to ensure that problems are detected in time to take corrective action.

Work Organisation

(1) I always keep all relevant materials, like diary, computer, working files, telephone, calculator, telephone directory and dictation machine, close to my work area.

(2) I ensure that my team members get necessary resources well in time so that they complete their tasks as scheduled.

(3) I do not allow crowding of my desk and keep it clear except the material needed to handle the task being worked on.

(4) I record at one place everything I have to do or remember.

(5) I do not start another task until I finish the task in hand.

Self-Discipline

(1) I plan each day with clear goals and keep it visible at all times.

(2) I set deadlines for every task for myself and my team.

(3) I ask for regular progress reports on all tasks.

(4) I keep a check on the progress of each task every day.

(5) I do not interrupt others on matters that can wait.

Saying "No"

(1) If I am asked to do some unreasonable thing or perform a task that someone else should, I say "no" without being offensive.

(2) I encourage my team members to tell me if my requests are unreasonable and would interfere with the tasks they are doing, and to suggest reasonable alternatives.

(3) I support my team members when they say "no" to unreasonable requests.

(4) I use many alternatives to saying "yes"

automatically when someone asks if I have "a minute".

(5) If I realise that I should not have said "yes" to the request made to me, I immediately tell the person that I had made a mistake and explain the reasons why I should say "no".

Procrastination

(1) If I have to put off a task, I set up the next deadline for myself, including a starting time.

(2) I keep a watch for procrastination in my team, and help them overcome it.

(3) If I face the problem of procrastination, I 'go public' by announcing my deadline and ask others to remind me if I ignore it.

(4) I practise self-rewards when progressing toward a deadline.

(5) If I am thinking of postponing the decision thinking that I may go wrong, I remind myself of the advantage of a fast decision.

Meetings

(1) If the purpose is not clear, I don't call a meeting, and I resist attending such meetings.

(2) My meetings have agendas and each item is allotted for discussion.

(3) When I call a meeting I ensure that it starts and ends on time.

(4) For those whom the full meeting is not important, they are encouraged to attend only the part applicable to them.

(5) If topics that aren't on the agenda are raised, I suggest putting them on the agenda for the next meeting so that everyone comes prepared.

Managing Paperwork

(1) Paperwork is reduced by eliminating all unnecessary forms, reports and copies of correspondence.

(2) Files are updated on a regular basis so that necessary papers are retrieved in minimum possible time.

(3) A system for the weeding of files and papers has been established and is maintained.

(4) Excessive policies, procedures and other forms of red tape have been done away with.

(5) I have studied and practised speed-reading.

Completing Tasks
(1) If I am interrupted during the work, I do not postpone the work.

(2) When it is not possible to postpone, I leave the work in the hands of someone who can complete it, or in a state where I can pick it up with minimum delay after the interruption has ended.

(3) Since cluttered desk provides constant interruptions, I practise keeping my desk clear except for the task I am working on.

(4) I take steps to control noise and visual distractions in my work environment.

(5) I have a system for screening telephone calls, unannounced-visitors, and uninvited paperwork.

Socialising
(1) I keep the door of my office closed to avoid unnecessary visitors. However, I make sure that those who have business to do, do not return without seeing me.

(2) I have developed techniques for terminating conversations without offending the other person.

(3) I do not encourage socialising situations, except

when appropriate, by having calls and visitors screened professionally.

(4) I ensure that location and position of desks are planned to minimise socialising.

Managing Information

(1) I organise in such a way that the information needed for decision making and planning strategies are available to my staff and me.

(2) I convene regular meetings for discussions with my team to ensure that they are properly informed on all aspects of the task they are involved in.

(3) When appropriate, I call brief meetings to coordinate the progress of the work with my team members.

(4) When necessary information sought by me is not provided, I talk to the person concerned and explain to him the importance of getting the information. If not successful, I approach my boss, or to the withholding party's boss with a request for assistance.

(5) I do not allow requests for irrelevant information.

Managing Travel

(1) When the possibility of travel arises, I consider the alternatives such as telephoning persons concerned, a teleconference with those involved with the task, writing to all relevant persons, or inviting the person to come to me.

(2) Before going on tour, I plan my travel. I examine the purpose of the tour carefully and list all materials necessary to accomplish the purpose.

(3) I pack materials for use en route in my briefcase for easy access.

(4) My itinerary includes all travel destinations, names of key people with phone numbers in case of travel delays, appointment times, locations and purposes.

(5) Before leaving, I discuss with my team what each one is expected to do by my return.

Now give marks to every ranking with the help of the following score table. If your marks are above 15, your time management is excellent; if it is more than 10 but less than 15, your rating is average; and below 10 is poor.

1. Almost never 0
2. Sometimes 1
3. Half the time 2
4. Usually 3
5. Always 4

Now you know where you stand. Improve your time management if your score is low. Maintain it if you are above 15.